How to Speak Husband

I owe a great debt of gratitude to my editorial advisor, Mr. Matthew Sheehy, who has labored countless hours to make my thoughts and my heart clear to my readers. Matthew Sheehy was born in New York City. He graduated from the SUNY College of Environmental Science and Forestry at Syracuse University in 1997 with a B.S. in chemistry. He then attended Duke University in Durham, North Carolina, with the intention of earning a Ph.D. in chemistry. Upon being called to the ministry under the preaching of Dr. Rick Finley at Fellowship Baptist Church, he left Duke University with an M.S. degree and moved to Northwest Indiana. He began attending the First Baptist Church of Hammond, Indiana, and Hyles-Anderson College in 2000. Matthew graduated from Hyles-Anderson in 2003 with a master's degree in pastoral theology. He has served as a Bible teacher and as an academic advisor at Hammond Baptist High School. Matthew and his wife, Amy, are the parents of one child. They now reside in Crown Point, Indiana.

Dedication

Affectionately dedicated to the married couples of First Baptist Church of Hammond. Thank you for striving alongside of me as we lay a foundation for the generation coming after us to build upon.

I love being your shepherd.

COPYRIGHT © 2010
Hyles Publications

1st Printing – March 2010

ISBN: 978-0-9819603-3-3

All Scripture quotations are from the King James Bible.

All rights reserved. If you would like to print any portion of this book, please contact Hyles Publications for written permission.

CREDITS
Project Manager: Dr. Bob Marshall
Assistant: Rochelle Chalifoux
Transcription: Cyndilu Marshall
Page Design and Layout: Linda Stubblefield
Proofreading: Rena Fish, Jane Grafton,
Julie Richter, and Maria Sarver

To order additional books by Dr. Jack Schaap,
please contact:
HYLES PUBLICATIONS
507 State Street
Hammond, Indiana 46320
www.hylespublications.com
e-mail: info@hylespublications.com

About the Author

$\mathcal{D}$r. Jack Schaap is the senior pastor of First Baptist Church of Hammond, Indiana, recognized as one of the largest congregations in America. First Baptist Church has the largest children's and teens' ministries in America. He has a B.S., an M.Ed., and a D.D. from Hyles-Anderson College in Crown Point, Indiana.

Pastor Schaap superintends more than 3,000 young people attending five separate, private Christian schools, including one in China and one in Ghana, whose operation is overseen by First Baptist Church. Pastor Schaap is the chancellor of Hyles-Anderson College, a private Bible college which First Baptist Church operates for the purpose of training preachers, missionaries, and Christian educators. For more than 20 years, he preached 35 yearly meetings to tens of thousands of teenagers.

Dr. Schaap is the author of 17 books and several pamphlets.

Dr. Schaap has been married to his wife Cindy since 1979, and they have two adult children who serve in the ministries of First Baptist Church.

Table of Contents

Introduction 9

Section One —
Defining and Translating the Roles in Marriage

1. Defining Your Role as a Wife 15

2. Defining the Roles of Your Husband 33

3. Practical Ideas to Help Your Husband
   Fulfill His Roles as a Man 51

Section Two —
Translating the Needs of Your Husband

4. The Basic Needs of Your Husband:
   A Wife Who Respects
   His Masculinity .67

5. The Basic Needs of Your Husband:
   A Wife Who Respects Him and
   Believes in Him as a Leader 77

6. The Basic Needs of Your Husband:
   A Wife Who Will Continue to Develop
   Inward and Outward Beauty 89

7. The Basic Needs of Your Husband:
   A Wife Who Can Lovingly Appeal
   to Him When He Is Wrong and
   Can Wisely Respond to Those
   Who Question Him 97

8. The Basic Needs of Your Husband:
   A Wife Who Is Grateful for All
   He Has Done and Is Doing for Her 101

9. The Basic Needs of Your Husband:
   A Wife Who Will Be Praised
   by Other People 107

10. The Basic Needs of Your Husband:
    A Wife With the Meekness
    to Meet His Needs 109

Introduction

*I*mmigration from Mexico is a hot topic in America. Some people argue that if immigrants come from Mexico, then they should learn English instead of trying to change the American culture. This book is not meant to raise the issue of immigration, but the example is similar to a root problem in marriage.

A husband and wife are like foreign immigrants coming to a new land. He comes to the land of Marriage speaking Husband, and she comes to the land of Marriage speaking Wife. The two languages sound similar, but the same words don't always have the same meanings in the two languages. The way a word is said in Husband is not the way it is interpreted in Wife and vice versa. A common expression of concern in the language of Wife might be a challenge to war in the language of Husband.

The differences between the languages of Husband and Wife are like the differences between American and British English. If an Englishman said, "I'm going to give Mrs. Smith a ring," he would mean that he was going to call Mrs. Smith on the telephone. If your husband said, "I'm going to give Mrs. Smith a ring," you would assume that he was giving her a piece of jewelry that is a symbol of his love and affection for her. You would be angry and jealous; you would worry that he is leaving you. Both men used the same words, but the meaning was different because of the culture.

"When men and women agree, it is only in their conclusions; their reasons are always different."

– George Santayana

Marriage is above all a representation of the Lord Jesus Christ and His church. If there is one message that the church needs to get across to the world, it is the love of Jesus Who died so men and women can be saved. The message is poorly displayed in many Christian marriages throughout our country. Lost souls misunderstand the Gospel just like people of different languages cannot comprehend each other.

Christian couples should be experts at building good marriages; it ought to be second nature. I want you to be

Introduction | *11*

exceedingly brilliant when it comes to building a marriage. It takes more than a desire and passion to build a good marriage.

The first step that I want you and your husband to take is the step of understanding each other. Evaluate if you understand your role as a wife by answering the following questions.

- As a wife, do you know the role God made for you to fulfill?
- As a wife, do you have Biblical expectations for yourself and for your husband?
- Do you know what roles God expects your husband to fulfill?
- Do you know how you are supposed to help him fulfill those roles?
- When you are annoyed by statements from your husband, do you truly understand what he is trying to express?
- Do you consider what he is saying from the perspective of being a woman?

"Keep in mind that the better you understand what you want and why you want it, the better your chances will be of acquiring it."

– Fred Jandt

Most wives haven't considered these questions. Most wives

could not define their role or the role of their husband. If a wife cannot define those roles, then she surely does not know how she is to fulfill those roles, nor how to help her husband fulfill his roles. Christians preach to the world, "Be like me," when they don't even know what they are supposed to be. Christian couples should have the most exemplary marriages in the world because they should operate according to God's principles.

> "To effectively communicate, we must realize that we are all different in the way we perceive the world and use this understanding as a guide to our communication with others."
>
> – Anthony Robbins

Genesis records the events that occurred when men put their minds together and started building a tower in Babel. God saw that men could build a tower that would "reach unto Heaven" because they were on the same page. He defeated their attempts by confounding their language. God knew that if people could not speak the same language, then they could not build something together. Because God chose to confound their language, we could safely conclude that a common language is the great tool to working together.

You and your husband cannot build a great marriage that will "reach unto heaven" until you speak the same language. *How to Speak Husband* is a tool to help you answer some of these vital questions about your role as a wife and your husband's role as your partner. When God saw the work at the tower of Babel, He said, *"...nothing will be restrained from them..."* because they were on the same page speaking the same language. You and your husband could have a powerful marriage where nothing would be withheld from you if you could translate the language of your husband and master the language that you should be speaking as a wife.

Chapter One

Defining Your Role as a Wife

As you define your role as a wife, it is best to look at the Bible and understand God's intentions for you in this role instead of trying to work through the modern day mumbo-jumbo and the mess that it has created. I will not include all of the Bible verses in this text, but I recommend that you read the first two chapters of Genesis and Ephesians 5. In this chapter, it is not my desire to give my opinion; it is my desire to expose how the Bible defines your role as a woman.

Please do not misunderstand this chapter. A skeptical person will read this chapter and say that I am down on women. I am not down on women. Ask my wife if I am down on women. Read her books and see if she feels that way. I am in favor of women assuming the role for which God created them. I am also for men being fulfilled in their role. Please read through this whole book and see the entire picture. I know that your husband might be lacking in his fulfillment as your husband. I promise that I am addressing that in the companion book. For now, though, I am giving you a short Bible lesson on your role as a wife before we discuss translating between the languages of Husband and Wife. You must choose whether or not you will be strong enough to be the wife that God wants you to be.

"You must choose whether or not you will be strong enough to be the wife that God wants you to be."

– Dr. Jack Schaap

The greatest challenge for a wife is fulfilling her husband's greatest need as described in Ephesians 5. If you want to know what your husband wants more than anything else and conquer the greatest challenge for a wife, then you need to understand Ephesians 5:21-24. *"Submitting yourselves one to another in the fear of God. Wives, submit yourselves unto your own husbands, as unto the Lord. For the husband is the head of the wife, even as Christ is the head of the church: and he is the saviour of the body. Therefore as the church is subject unto Christ, so let the wives be to their own husbands in every thing."*

The Bible says that the husband is the head of the wife. In our society, we accept a man's being in charge of certain areas, but God says that he is not just in charge of an area; he is in charge over the wife. The Bible makes that position very clear. God appointed you to be your husband's wife.

A father may say to his daughter's suitor, "I give my blessing to you to marry my daughter," but that father cannot appoint the headship of his son-in-law. God gives a husband that headship.

The ultimate decision that is made in the relationship between a husband and wife is that the wife will decide who leads her. Every other decision and problem will stem from that one decision you will make as a wife. You essentially have to decide if you will or will not submit to God's design.

Husband leadership is a great rub in marriage. God's Biblical design is not in accord with many of the excuses that men and women give for their marital problems. The struggle in marriage is deciding who will be in charge.

Certainly, there are problems with husbands who will not lead or who have left for a while, but a husband's level of character does not change the level of God's challenge to his wife.

We are so quick to tell God why we cannot obey His words. Many ladies have piled up excuses like firewood on why they cannot follow their husbands. Nonetheless,

God said there is one thing the man is in charge of, and that is his wife. The greatest challenge for a woman is to say, "I will make everyone know—especially my husband—that he leads me." Those are hard words for women of the twenty-first century.

The wife who fails at submitting to her husband's leadership has failed at the greatest challenge of being a wife. If your husband doesn't know that he is the boss, then you are failing as a wife because *"…the husband is the head of the wife, even as Christ is the head of the church.…"*

I preach at churches around the country. I have seen many churches where I felt the people needed to get reconnected to Jesus Christ and figure out that He is in charge of the church. I have seen some churches where if Christ was in charge, then no one knew it. I have seen churches that were led by a mouthy woman or by a very stubborn, incorrigible man. I have seen churches run by teenagers setting the standards and forcing their parents and adults out of power. I have seen churches that are run by the Super Bowl. I have seen churches that are run by anything other than Jesus Christ, and none of those churches thrive.

If a church cannot thrive when Christ is not the head, why would you expect your marriage to thrive if your husband is not the head? Even worse is the fact

Defining Your Role as a Wife | *19*

that you are the reason why your husband cannot be the head. Every woman is capable of fighting with a man, but the point of marriage is not to express your ability to compete and dominate. The purpose of marriage is to show the world a relationship similar to Christ and His church. God's design as you fulfill that purpose includes your husband's being the head and your being submissive to his authority. If you question why that is, then I can only answer that God made it that way.

The Bible tells us in I Timothy chapters 2 and 3 that we will know when Christ is the head of the church. The illustration of headship is the local church because the husband is the head like Christ is the head. The wife is to submit as the church submits to Christ. If we look at that illustration and see the parallels, it should be easy for people to manifest their roles. I Timothy 2:8-12 says, *"I will therefore that men pray every where, lifting up holy hands, without wrath and doubting. In like manner also, that women adorn themselves in modest apparel, with shamefacedness and sobriety; not with broided hair, or gold, or pearls, or costly array; But (which becometh women professing godliness) with good works. Let the woman learn in silence with all subjection. But I suffer not a woman to teach, nor to usurp authority over the man, but to be in silence."*

The first way to determine if a woman is submissive is if she is not publicly vocal in her disagreements

with the church. The Bible says in I Timothy 2 that a church is properly run by the headship of Jesus Christ when men assume the leadership positions. When the Bible says, "...*men pray every where*...," it means that men are leading in prayer or leading the church. The passage specifically says that issues of the church need to be addressed by the men and not the women. That idea is repeated later in the passage when it says that women are not to be vocal in the church. The picture in I Timothy is of a church where women are not pushing to have their voice heard.

I have preached in churches where women have approached me and said, "Now let me tell you something. That may work where you come from, but we don't want that kind of preaching here."

I always cut them off and say, "Ma'am, I don't care what you think." I am not very polite to them because the Bible says that this woman's speaking up is a crucial sign that Christ is not the head of the church. I don't work for her; I work for Christ. Nobody is going to insult my Boss. If a man came to me and questioned what I said, I would be glad to discuss it with him. Men have a right to pray or to address or petition the problem.

I am not saying that a woman cannot come to a man of God with a question or problem. When a woman comes to me for a question, I will say, "That is an excellent question. Bring your husband here, and I will answer that question for you." I do that because when a woman disconnects from her husband—whether it is in the home or in the church—then she has begun the cycle of a lack of subjection. The couple is confusing their roles, and they are going to turn the cart upside down.

When the divorce rate in so-called Bible-believing churches is approximating that of the world, it tells me that something is horrifically wrong in our churches. The one thing that is wrong is we do not have Christ as the head. We have lost the orientation of headship. The influence of a church that is not led by Christ has spread to the marriage within the Christian homes.

Your children should know who the boss of your home is without anyone ever having to tell them. Your actions towards your husband should be such that the children know that you look to him for leadership. In your own house, no one should ever have to be reminded who the leader is. If that never has to be said, then it is obvious that you are a submissive wife.

Submission is important; it goes back to the book of Genesis. Before the fall of man, there is only one reference to Adam's speaking in the first two chapters of Genesis. It is an indirect reference of Adam's naming the animals. God told Adam to name the animals whatever he chose. The name that Adam chose would be the name of the animal. Whatever Adam said, God agreed on it with him.

Just as God accepted what Adam said, He accepts what a husband says because he is the one in charge. God will hold your husband accountable for the things for which you submit to him. If God accepts what your husband says at face value, then he does not expect you to do any less. When you are not subject to your own husband, you are defying the example of God and the commands of God.

You might think, "What if I don't believe that? What if I don't believe what my husband says?" That issue is addressed in Matthew 16:15-19, which says, *"He saith unto them, But whom say ye that I am? And Simon Peter answered and said, Thou art the Christ, the Son of the living God. And Jesus answered and said unto him, Blessed art thou, Simon Barjona: for flesh and blood hath not revealed it unto thee, but my Father which is in heaven. And I say also unto thee, That thou art Peter, and upon this rock I will build my church; and the gates of hell shall not prevail against it. And **I will give unto thee** the keys of the kingdom of heaven: and whatsoever thou shalt bind on earth shall be bound in heaven: and whatsoever **thou** shalt loose on earth shall be loosed in heaven."*

In this passage Jesus was talking to the disciples. After being asked if they knew Who Jesus was, Peter

Defining Your Role as a Wife | 23

alone replied that Jesus was *"the Christ, the Son of the living God."* By his answer Peter understood that Jesus was the ultimate authority. Jesus agreed that He had the ultimate Authority and then told Peter that He was commissioning authority on earth to Peter. Jesus said that He had decided to accept what Peter wanted to do on earth. If Peter bound it, Jesus bound it. If Peter loosed it, Jesus loosed it.

God gives the approval stamp to what a husband says and expects the wife to obey it. God does not command the wife to obey all men but to obey that one man who is her husband. Ladies should certainly be courteous, polite, and kind to other men, but there is only one man they are commanded to obey. Biblical submission is not all women being placed under all men. Biblical submission is one woman following the command to be subject to her one husband.

The Bible uses two military terms, *submit* and *subject*, to describe how to behave toward your husband. These words are military terms of "rank" and "file." A wife is to organize herself as to march in rank behind her husband in the cadence that he establishes.

If you say, "Well, then I am nothing but a slave," you are mistaken because the church is not a slave to Christ. Nowhere in the Bible is the church called the slave of Christ, but it is called the bride of Christ.

24 | How to Speak Husband

Someone wisely said that Eve was not taken from Adam's foot to be walked on, nor was she taken from his head to rule over him. She was taken from his rib to be his companion— near to his heart.

You are not a slave to your husband. Military men who go through boot camp do not consider themselves slaves of the military; they consider themselves obedient to the military. There might be a moment in their early days of service when they feel like a slave, but that is not the case. The husband that you chose is the man whom God commands you to follow. As long as he is alive, he is your superior in command, just like everyone in the military has a superior. You can have excuses, but the military accepts no excuses. Until you can follow your husband—even if he is a weak leader—there is no sense in talking about excuses because you have yet to try God's method. Perhaps you should have proven his capabilities and worthiness as a leader prior to marrying him?!

Your excuse might be that your husband isn't a good leader, but you still are commanded to follow your husband. Quality of leadership differs from empowerment of leadership. You must empower your husband. When a child comes to you and asks what to do in certain situations, you should say, "That is a great question, Son. I am so glad you asked me. Your father is the wisest man in the world. Please ask him."

If the child replies, "I asked him, and he said to ask you," then you should say, "I will talk to your father; he will make the decision, and I will relay his decision to you." There is a way to elicit that response from your husband.

You should go to your husband and say, "What would you like for me to tell your son?"

Your husband might say, "Tell him what you want to tell him."

You should say, "What would you prefer I tell him? Would you like me to tell him this or this?" Lay out options for your husband and coax him into being a leader.

Invent lots of plans, ideas, opinions, and options, but let the person in charge pick them. If your husband says, "I like that idea," then implement it. It doesn't put you in charge, but it helps your husband be the leader.

Your excuse for not following your husband might be that your husband doesn't have a purpose, but you still are commanded to follow your husband.

Your excuse for not following your husband might be that you don't like his direction, but you still are commanded to follow your husband.

Your excuse for not following your husband might be that he doesn't have enough wisdom, but you still are commanded to follow your husband.

Have you even tried following God's plan for being a wife?

Does your family know that your husband is in charge of you?

If I called your mother and asked her what she thought about your following your husband, would she give me a list of your husband's weaknesses? Have you filled your mother's mind with a list of what your husband doesn't do well? Have you told your father and mother that your husband is not worthy of submission? Can you think of any place in the Bible where it says you have to define the worthiness of your husband's leadership before you decide to submit? It's not there.

God never commands you to first figure out if your husband is worthy of following. God simply says to follow him.

Perhaps you say that living with him is Hell on earth. Do you know what Hell is? Hell is a place filled with people who pointed at Jesus and said, "We will not have that Man to rule over us." Your home will be the same if you don't submit. Your home might be hell because the people in it are pointing at your husband and saying, "We will not have that man to rule over us."

When you won't submit to your husband, you are shaking your fist at God and saying, "You don't know what You are doing!" You have your excuses, but I have

Defining Your Role as a Wife | **27**

learned that we have to first deal with following the commands; then we can deal with the exceptions. When God said that wives must be in subjection to their own husbands as the church subjects itself to Christ, He meant **YOU**. Until you are willing to accept that statement for what it says, you will not fulfill the role for which God made you. You can make excuses, but if all of the excuses are valid, then at what point will any husband love his wife and any wife be subject unto her husband?

The second way to determine if a woman submits to her husband is through her dress. As the Bible addresses the subject of the church in I Timothy, it suddenly mentions how women dress. The Bible teaches that the church is properly organized and submissive to Christ when the men bring up the issues, the women say nothing, and when the women look like they are in submission to authority.

Are you wearing your hair in a certain style because you want it that way, or did you seek your husband's opinion? Do you wear what you wear to church to please your friends or to please your husband? How does a recruit submit his hairstyle to the Marine Corps? Marines all have the same haircut because it is a symbol of whom they follow.

The greatest temptation for a woman as she fulfills her role is to control or change her husband. This temptation happens when a husband won't lead like a wife desires. You must resist the temptation to usurp his power.

Lack of creativity, lack of thought, and lack of using a brain are why bad marriages exist. A bad marriage is a lazy marriage. A bad marriage is a marriage that does not want to work and say, "How can I get this done?" Having a great marriage takes a lot of work from a wife.

Submission is a great challenge because you have to be creative in ways to get your husband to lead. You must devise ways to respect his position and to make him feel like he is in charge. When your needs are not being fulfilled, it is tempting to control or change your husband so that you feel fulfilled. It is a great achievement to be content within the context of your life. If you are content with what God has given to you, it is because you have worked hard.

If you have not worked hard at your marriage, then you have worked hard at rationalizing why your husband doesn't make you happy. If you think that your husband's duty is to serve you and therefore make you happy, then you will not be happy because that is not his duty. Your husband was not commanded by God to work all day and then come home and serve you.

Serving is a choice made by great people who simply

want to get the job done. You might have an adequate marriage because your husband is a truly great man who has accepted the challenge of serving you to keep you from harping all the time. You might have an adequate marriage because you have accepted the challenge of serving your husband so that he will not gripe all of the time. Many couples don't work together as a team, and the challenge in marriage is to find contentment instead of fulfillment and advancement.

Women look for excuses. The excuses replace the answers to the questions to which they cannot find answers. The questions are:

1. Why does God hate me?
2. Why doesn't God love me?
3. Why do I feel so left out of my husband's life?
4. Why is my family my only security? When they leave me, why do I feel abandoned and neglected?

The companion book talks to the husband about his role in answering these questions for the wife, but I want to address the most common excuse ladies use for their problems. The excuse is the menstrual cycle and the menopausal phase of life. These are certainly times of mood swings, but they do not excuse behavior. These times of the month or times of life do not **cause** a person's behavior; they simply **magnify** what is already there.

Many women suppress their negative feelings and maintain a certain decorum because it is expected of them for three weeks out of the month and the first 40 years of life. When there are biological changes and mood changes, the emotions are magnified, and the nerves go right to the surface. What has always been suppressed comes to the surface. Anger during these times isn't caused by a cycle; the cycles reveals what is already there.

Of course, you can say, "But you've never been there." That's true, but I have to reply that there is nothing in the Bible about having a biological excuse for your behavior. If that's your excuse, then you will never fix and improve your marriage. Ephesians 4:26 says, *"Be ye angry, and sin not...."* Thus, you do not have to sin when times are hard, or God would not say that you are able to refrain from the sin.

Will you get to a point where you can lay your excuses aside that keep you from fulfilling your role? Jesus Christ won't excuse your lack of Christianity because you had a hysterectomy or a tubal ligation. He will still want to know if you obeyed His Bible. Thus, we want to get down to where the Bible is and obey it. Your husband needs to do that as a man, and you need to do that as a wife.

Defining Your Role as a Wife

I am asking you to put aside your excuses. Your marriage needs improving, and excuses do nothing except concede defeat to the problems. Would you agree with God that your chief role is to submit to your husband and to be his helper? If you can agree to that, then the rest of this book will help you to fulfill that role.

Chapter Two

Defining the Roles of Your Husband

As we define your husband's role, it is best to look at the Bible and understand God's intentions for him in this role just as we did for your role. I am not going to include all of the Bible verses in this text, but I recommend that you read the first two chapters of Genesis. In this chapter, it is not my desire to give my opinion; it is my desire to expose how the Bible defines your husband's role as a man.

Genesis 1 records that God created everything. Genesis 2 backtracks and gives more information about two particular creations of God: man and the Garden. These two must be important if God took the time to address them in more detail. The text says that God gave man four things.

1 **God gave man life.**
Genesis 2:4-7 tells the story of God's creating Adam. Genesis 2:8-14 tells the story of God's creating the Garden. Verse 8 describes the first relationship between Adam and the Garden. God made the Garden, and He put Adam in that Garden. *"And the LORD God planted a garden eastward in Eden; and there he put the man whom he had formed."* (Genesis 2:8)

2 **God gave man a purpose.**
Verse 15 then ties these two important creations together and defines your husband's purpose as a man. *"And the LORD God took the man, and put him into the garden of Eden to dress it and to keep it."* (Genesis 2:15)

Man's role in the garden was to dress it and to keep it. When the Bible says that Adam dressed the garden, it means that he worked and served in it. Webster's 1828 dictionary defines *dress* as "to put something in a straight line or order, to put things in order, and specifically, to till or cultivate." Adam tilled the land and planted seeds in straight rows as we see farmers do today. When the Bible says that Adam kept the garden, it means that he protected it, guarded it, and generally took care of its needs.

3 **God gave man boundaries.**
God created your husband, gave him a role, and gave him some boundaries for playing that role. God

gave Adam a role in the Garden, and He also gave him some boundaries in Genesis 2:16 and 17 that define that role. *"And the LORD God commanded the man, saying, Of every tree of the garden thou mayest freely eat: But of the tree of the knowledge of good and evil, thou shalt not eat of it: for in the day that thou eatest thereof thou shalt surely die."*

4. **God gave man a helper to accomplish his role.** God created your husband, gave him a role, gave him some boundaries for playing his role, and gave you to your husband as a helper. God created Adam, gave him a purpose in caring for the Garden, defined his boundaries of what he could eat, and He then gave Eve to Adam to be his helper. *"And the LORD God said, It is not good that the man should be alone; I will make him an help meet for him."* (Genesis 2:18)

People bristle over defined roles because they feel confined. When I counsel with couples, I define their separate roles as a husband and a wife. Marital problems ultimately occur when either spouse says, "I will not play my role." A wife will never improve, grow, or heal her marriage until she finds contentment and joy in fulfilling the role that God has given to her and until she allows her husband to fulfill his roles.

The remainder of this chapter will be devoted to defining your husband's roles as a man. Before he became your husband, he was a man. Thus, if you will properly translate Husband to Wife, you must first understand his culture.

ROLE #1:
Man was made to dominate.

Your husband has a subconscious desire to dominate or control his environment. That is how God fashioned him. Genesis 1:26-28 records that God said that man would have dominion over the earth and that which is therein. Domination is in the genes of a man. However politically correct the world becomes, a man cannot escape his innate nature to dominate. God put a man in the Garden by himself and said, "Run the show, Adam." Adam was empowered by God to run his environment.

Your husband probably hates when you say, "Maybe we should stop for directions." That sentence irks him because when he is driving, he is dominating his environment; that environment is the car. Way back when he was in the seed of Adam, God told him to control his environment, so he naturally does not like when you tell him how to control the car.

Teenage boys struggle with being accepted as a man by their parents, and the struggle can continue with their wife when they get married. I am using a stereotype for example, but when you suggest that he stop for directions, he probably will not stop. I don't deny that a wife might have a good idea, but before robbing a man of his manhood, be sure that you want a little boy for your spouse. You can demand your way, but he will resort to being a five-year-old boy, and you might resort to receiving alimony checks. The day might come when he walks out and doesn't come home. Your demanding your way is not an excuse for that behavior. My point is that men love to dominate, and there will be a problem when you try to dominate him.

I love being the pastor of the First Baptist Church of Hammond; it is the environment in which God gave me some control. People like to offer their advice on how I should do my job. I am kind to them, but deep down I don't want their advice because I am a man and want to dominate the job that God gave me to do.

Men have an attitude that you might think is cocky, arrogant, and self-righteous. I call it God's design for a man. Your husband should find a certain confidence in saying, "This is my house. This is my wife. These are my kids. This is my car, and I like it with the muffler hanging off. It gives me identity. I will fix it when I am good and ready." You should respect his manliness.

Men have an attitude of domination. You can call it cocky. You can call it arrogant. You can call it self-righteous. You can call it anything you want, but the Bible calls it God's plan that a man dominates his world.

Role #2:
A man must define himself.

A man defines himself by his work. A man is what a man does. When you and your husband were falling in love and got engaged, you might have reached the peak of your romance. You believed that he would always be so romantic and thoughtful, but the romance usually falls off from that point. At the peak of his romantic output, he was buying rings, setting up elaborate proposals, kneeling in a restaurant, and making a total jerk of himself in front of a lot of people. He swooned over you.

A Proposal of Marriage	
Translation in Wife	*Translation in Husband*
An extremely romantic evening that culminates in the offer to be the object of his affection and desire for decades to come	The moment I obtained permanent companionship and no longer needed to pursue her.

Suppose I had asked you at the moment you were engaged, "What are you going to do with your life?" You would have answered, "I am going to be a wife," because women define themselves by their relationships.

Suppose I had walked up to your husband at the

same point and said, "Sir, what are you going to do with your life?" There is not a man in the world that would have said, "I am going to be a husband," because men do not define themselves by their relationships.

Men define themselves by their work. I am a pastor. I am a teacher. I am a counselor. I am an author. My father was a construction worker; he was also a businessman. Your husband has a job title, and that title is how he likely defines himself. Our modern era has confused masculinity by mingling the genders and adding titles and ranks to jobs that make men fight to say, "I'm as good as you are." That is all a bunch of modern humanism that needs to be ignored by Bible-believing people.

Regardless of our culture, a man must define himself. He defines himself by his work. Simply put, a man is what a man does.

ROLE #3:
A man is a protector.

Men have a subconscious desire to protect; they love it. Your husband wants to protect you. Men don't just want to protect their family, however; they also want to protect their neighbor.

A man will protect his neighbor's house as aggressively as he would protect his own house; it is an instinct. If your husband saw someone being abused or injured, he would not first ask himself, "Is there any danger to me if I get involved? What will be the repercussions if I help this lady, knowing my wife is jealous?" He doesn't care. He jumps out of the car, grabs a weapon, and beats whatever person or animal is abusing another.

Your husband is willing to defend anything. You need to understand that your husband is a protector by nature, not just a protector of you. If you do not understand this, you will develop unnecessary jealousy. The desire to protect is related to the desire to dominate. If someone injures something that is your husband's, that person has stepped on his turf, dominated it, and trespassed upon the first role.

Role #4:

Men compete to overcome their natural weaknesses.

Men are competitive. Something inside of a man says, "I can beat that." However much money your husband made last year, he would like to make more this year. When he fails, he says, "If it weren't for such and such, I would have made more." Men believe that they are better than what they appear to be. Men are always trying to say, "You don't even know how good I am. In fact, watch me."

The dares are always with the guys and not with the girls. I realize there are some tomboys who can out wrestle their husband and embarrass him, but that's not typical. When men get together, they don't say, "Hey Bob, so do you and your wife have a meaningful relationship?" They don't say, "John, how is your boss? Is he dealing with the emotional crisis of his son's having leukemia?" Men don't talk about those things.

When men get together and talk about themselves, they are quantifying their greatness. Men care how many points are on their buck. If your husband's friend got a six-point buck, then he wants an eight-point buck. Men brag that their shift made the greatest number of widgets in the history of Widgets, Inc. It doesn't matter what they make; what matters is that they are the best at what they do. Your husband is a man; he feels the same way. Men always want to do better and be more productive. That's what they discuss.

When I get together with other pastors, we talk about how our churches are doing. We talk about our attendance numbers. When I am with pastors, none of them have ever initially asked me, "How is your marriage, and how is Mrs. Schaap?" They might ask about my wife eventually, but men first talk about production because that is what men care about. Your husband only asks other men about their success so that he can then tell them why his success is better.

When you talk to another lady, you genuinely ask

42 | How to Speak Husband

each other, "How is your husband? How is the family?"

You don't ask, "Why do you want to know?" You say, "Let me tell you about it. He is having a little bit of trouble with psoriasis, and we are using 'Scalp X.' What do you recommend?" Men don't care about those issues.

The Hebrew word for man is *adam*, and it means "to lift up and overcome." The very label that God put on His creation was the label of an overcomer. When God made your husband, He was saying, "Watch this man overcome everything. Watch him go to work." Once God blew breath into Adam's nostrils, Adam went to work.

Proverbs 20:29 says, *"The glory of young men is their strength: and the beauty of old men is the gray head."* Younger men find their glory in their strength and productivity. Older men don't care about their beauty until they are too old to be productive. They still have a mentality to do something great, but men never really get that touchy-feely ability until they have reached the age where most everything doesn't work anymore. Then they are old, and everything seems beautiful to them.

Old men will say, "We sat in our La-Z-Boy chairs, and we read old issues of *Reader's Digest* together." Young men don't do that; young men are physically competitive. Grandpas start living vicariously through their grandchildren when they realize that they can't compete physically. Grandfathers want their grandson to go to college on a scholarship. They want their sons and grandsons to excel in areas in which they could not excel. It is very natural and very right, and God designed it that way. Men are competitive.

ROLE #5:
Men develop a big picture.

Men are big-picture people; they focus on what will happen in the future. The entire area of Eden (not just the Garden) was about 500 miles from east to west and about 500 miles north to south. When God told Adam that it was his, I don't think that Adam thought that the land was too big for him.

As a pastor, I will never think that my church is big enough. It can always get bigger. Your husband's influence at work is never big enough for his manhood. He knows that he could always do more, even if the boss doesn't see the potential in him.

The gender of a child is determined at conception, but it does not begin to develop sexual-specific traits until a few weeks and months later. When boys begin to develop their masculine traits in the womb, the right half of the brain begins to enlarge; the left half shrinks, and the cord that connects the two snaps. Because of this, men tend to be dominated by one half of their brain more than the other. Most men are dominated by the right half of their brain, and this half tends to develop the big picture.

The right half of the brain enables people to perform athletically, have dexterity, and perform manual work. It is where people develop a competitive edge, logic, and the ability to explain. The left half of the brain enables us to be artistic, poetic, musical, and excel at some of the sciences. There is nothing feminine or masculine about those traits; it is a result of brain development.

Men can learn to develop both sides of their brain, but they generally do not. There is a stereotype of the male musician who is laughed at by the construction worker. The construction worker thinks that the pianist is a wimp, and he would like to break the piano in half with his hands. The chiding is often the result of the burly man's embarrassment at his inability to write a poem; he couldn't pronounce Chaucer if he saw it written and couldn't name a poem by the famous poet. The construction worker knows how to swing a hammer, though; he knows how to turn a wrench; he knows how to fix a gutter; he knows how to lay shingles. The point is that men want a big picture whether they are dominated by the left brain or the right brain.

For women, both halves of the brain are the same size, and there is a connection between the two. This is why women are better at having strengths resulting from

Defining the Roles of Your Husband | 45

the left and right brain. They really are a little more coordinated.

When your family goes on vacation, your husband wants to wake up at 3:59 a.m., load the car, and take off by 4:00 a.m. He is on a non-stop trip to Orlando. He doesn't care if the kids have to go to the bathroom. The only reason he will stop is the fact that the car doesn't have a big enough gas tank to drive non-stop to Orlando.

Your husband puts you through Hades to get to the vacation spot, and you need a vacation from going on vacation with him. A man can spend about three days on vacation, and then he is ready to go home because his big picture takes shape. There is no big picture on vacation. He wants to go home and get back to work where he produces things. He becomes mission-minded again after several days of vacation; he wants to go accomplish something.

Women often tend to see the immediate picture before they see the big picture. When it comes to vacation, you care more about the number of pairs of underwear that you have packed for your husband before you care about getting in the car and going to Orlando. Your husband is happy as long as he already has on a pair of underwear that he can wear into the chlorine-saturated swimming pool for washing each day. You care more about if you remembered your toothbrush than how many miles-per-gallon the car will get and calculating how many stops you will have to make based on the size of your fuel tank. Your husband knows that he can buy another toothbrush at the Walmart in Florida. If he exclusively planned and prepared for the vacations, the kids would not have anything to wear; they would never eat; and your little girl would still be wearing the same diaper at the end of the vacation. Most men just aren't as good at seeing the immediate picture because they focus on the big picture.

A Vacation	
Translation in Wife	*Translation in Husband*
Seven days of well-planned activity that exclusively includes your husband and children as well as a large quantity of quality time with the family	An annual event where I accomplish arriving so that I can accomplish returning to my normal life.

Role #6:

Men have a subconscious desire for companionship.

Men are more romantic than women. Neither you nor your husband would probably agree with that statement, but the romance he displayed in finding a companion outweighed any effort you have put forth to be romantic. He chased you, he asked you out, he paid for the dates, he bought the ring, and he might have planned the honeymoon.

Romance declines after the wedding because men achieved their goal. Men are goal-oriented. His goal was to get a companion; he obtained one, and he feels that he doesn't have to maintain that level of effort. He achieved his goal, so he stopped planning and imagining. Despite his goal orientation, he has a desire for companionship.

Men want companionship so that someone will notice how great they are. What a man likes is to have his buddy say, "I have to hand it to you; I have never seen anyone do that as well as you." They want recognition from their peer group. A man loves the little girl who walks up and says, "You are awesome." But more than that, he would do anything to have *his girl* say that he is awesome. Men want women to appreciate how incredibly good they are at what they do.

You are the one person whom your husband wants to impress; he wants you to recognize his greatness. When you tell him that he is great, he is ready to conquer Hell for you. Therein lies a fundamental point of great marital success: you need to recognize your husband's accomplishments. He doesn't really want anybody else's recognition since he found you. He won't seek recognition elsewhere if he is getting it at home.

Men will go to great lengths for a woman's approval. They will start a war, go to war, or end a war if their woman will say, "You're my hero." Men are pretty simple to figure out. If a woman tells a man he is wonderful, then he will jump through hoops for her.

Your husband might struggle with receiving praise due to an injured psyche because of mistakes made in the past by him or mistakes that people made in dealing with him. He wants the admiration, but he doesn't trust the words of the person who praises him. Perhaps he has been injured by an abusive home, a terrible example, or loved ones who have betrayed him. He might be skeptical.

You might be a wife who is trying to be his cheerleader. Perhaps he is telling you to be quiet because he doesn't believe your words. If your husband is like this, he believes that he is a failure, and he feels that people are patronizing him when they say kind words. If he has condemned himself or lashed out at you while you are trying to be his cheerleader, he is displaying the evidence of an unhealed wound; he has judged himself undeserving of the praise. He married you because he liked your praise, but now he dismisses it. The two of you are caught in a push-pull, and you need counsel because you are stuck between a rock and a hard place.

A Date	
Translation in Wife	*Translation in Husband*
A time spent establishing feelings and creating a deep, personal bond with my husband	A task necessary to make my wife want sexual intimacy

Men communicate to define who they are. Women communicate to bond with a person. You talk until you feel close. He talks until he has convinced another person that he is on his own turf, that it will be done his way, and until he feels like he has defined himself.

Men talk about how fast their car is, how fast they can paint the car, how fast they can drive the car, how fast they can fix the car, or how fast they can wash their car; they are just looking for something where they are better than another. Men talk about how big a gun they have and how many birds or deer they have shot. They brag that they shot a 12-point buck when they didn't even create the deer.

As a man, I am victim to the same thing. I have far too many times looked at a little spike-horned buck, pointed my rifle scope at it, and thought, "You are not even worth the bullet, you stupid little creature. I deserve you, and you deserve this bullet." I pulled the trigger and got an ego trip because I shot a deer that has four or five points on each side. Hunting isn't what makes men wonderful and important, but such things are how men sometimes judge their manhood. They then talk about what they did to define themselves.

Talking is an essential part of companionship, but men talk to do, not to feel. Women like to talk to establish feelings and not to accomplish a task. This area right here is why the sex life stinks for many couples. You want your husband to talk you into having sex. He just wants to have the action, and then he will talk about how wonderful it was. You have reached an impasse and one that this book might help you overcome.

The roles of your husband are roles that you must help him fulfill. You are his helper and completer. A wise wife will read these roles and consider how she can help her husband fulfill them so that he can accomplish the roles that God assigned to him. The remaining chapters offer practical ideas on how you can meet his needs in this area.

Chapter Three

Practical Ideas to Help Your Husband Fulfill His Roles as a Man

The last chapter was designed to help you understand your husband's God-given roles. An essential element of success in your marriage is that you help him to achieve these roles. Remember that you were made to be his helper. Now that you better understand his roles, I have included suggestions for how you can help him achieve success in those roles.

Idea #1:
Accept the fact that your husband's priority is his work and not his wife.

I can understand why that statement might upset a wife, but it would be worse if she didn't comprehend the

Bible truth about a man. God wrote the Bible. He tells us how to have a happy marriage, and He said that a wife is not her husband's defining characteristic. You were created for him; he was not created for you. *"Neither was the man created for the woman; but the woman for the man."* (I Corinthians 11:9)

If you badger your husband into exalting you above his work, you will have a very confused and frustrated man. Many marital problems are caused by a woman who does not believe this verse. God made men to work and women to help men accomplish that work. Your role is to help your husband succeed in what God told him to do. Your husband didn't define those roles; God did, so don't take it out on your husband.

Will you look at your husband and make him the object of your ministry to God? You can still walk hand in hand and watch the sunset, but you can't live a honeymoon life that only includes the two of you. At some point, your husband has to fulfill his ultimate desire to work and produce something. He wants to provide for you and protect you. Yes, he wants to love you, but above all of that, he wants to work. Remember that God made Adam to work before He made Eve to be his helper.

Idea #2:
Be your husband's cheerleader.

Pump up your husband; inflate his ego. Give him the confidence he needs so that he can do the great work that God has called him to do. In return you will receive great joy, satisfaction, and happiness. You and his job are not the opposing teams competing for your husband. You are on your husband's team; you cheer him to victory.

Your husband should hear you say, "Go for it!" He should hear you say, "I think that is a great idea," or, "I think you can do it," or "Believe in yourself because I believe in you."

Your husband needs to hear that you believe in him. These

"Behold the turtle. He makes progress only when he sticks his neck out."

– James B. Conan

simple words in the language of Wife are translated into Husband as words that inspire and give life to his dreams. Remind your husband how secure you feel when he is around. You can remind him by something as simple as asking him to remove the lid from a jar. He might know that you could remove it yourself, but he still likes the attention. When he twists it off, you should say something like, "Wow! You are strong. Are you as good in bed as you are with jars?" Make your husband feel like he is the stud of your life. Do it before someone else does.

> "Treat people as if they were what they ought to be and you help them to become what they are capable of being."
>
> – Johann Wolfgang von Goethe

If you don't want to tell your husband that he is wonderful, then who should tell him? Your husband is probably pretty good at what he does. There are people at work who believe in him, but he may not think that his wife believes in him. He doesn't need a woman walking up to him at work and saying, "You are our star employee." You shouldn't want another woman telling him that. He should be able to tell that woman that his wife already tells him that he is a star at home.

Give your husband the confidence he needs even if he fails. Isn't that what cheerleaders are for? Cheerleaders are to help, especially when a team or man is not performing well.

Idea #3:
Don't develop a nagging and complaining spirit.

The most destructive weapons in marriage are a nagging or complaining tongue and spirit. Nothing crushes a man's desire to dominate his world quite like a wife who possesses these destructive weapons. A man needs his wife to be the cheerleader, so nagging and complaining tell him that you don't believe in him.

"Remember not only to say the right thing in the right place, but far more difficult still, to leave unsaid the wrong thing at the tempting moment."

– Benjamin Franklin

God believed in Adam. God gave dominion over everything on the earth to men. Adam was instructed to name every living creature according to Genesis 2:19. Science has been studying these creatures for thousands of years and has yet to discover all of the animals that Adam named. Adam received total confidence from God even before he had a wife. God believed that Adam could do the job.

COMPLAINTS FROM A WIFE	
Translation in Wife	*Translation in Husband*
An attempt to get across her point after several attempts at subtle hints	My wife doesn't believe in me.

When God believes in a man, there is no limit to what that man can accomplish. When a wife also believes in her husband, she does not hinder his accomplishing God's plan. The ceiling over a husband's head is the complaining spirit of his wife. Perhaps you did not have a model home which illustrated how a wife should treat a husband, but you must look at the model that God sets forth in the Bible and develop a new idea of what your husband needs.

Idea #4:

Be a mother to the little boy inside of your husband, but not to the professional man that others know.

Every man is partially a little boy that never grew up. His nature that he possessed as a tiny tot stays with him. As his body grows up, his mind develops, and he begins his professional life. Still, he never loses the desire to play and explore.

When you hear your husband talking about a hunting trip or fishing trip or bowling, it would be good if you would come up to him and say, "Wow! That sounds like a great idea. You should do that." I'm not advocating that a husband always hang out with his buddies. Meeting up with other friends on a regular basis is unhealthy for a marriage. However, if your little boy wanted to go fishing at the creek, you would probably pack him a lunch and send him off. Why not do the same for your husband?

How would you feel if your husband gave you $500

for shopping? Suppose he overheard you discussing going to the mall with some of your friends on a Thursday night. Wouldn't you be thrilled if he told you that he thought your going shopping was a great idea and gave you some money? That is exactly how your husband would feel if you supported the little boy inside of him.

People have a nasty habit of forgetting that everyone—male and female—loves to be childlike. Unfortunately, the person who reminds us that the behavior is not permissible is usually our spouse. We are told to grow up, to act our age, and to knock it off. You might say, "But I am not married to a child." I think you are, and the art of being a good wife involves learning to deal with the little boy inside of your husband.

The Bible says you have to become as children, or you will not inherit the kingdom of heaven. It is my belief that we don't enter Heaven as adults; I think we enter as children. Adults are boring and incompetent. They are destroying America and the world. They kill each other, they start wars, they divorce, they hate, and they use vulgar language.

Children don't do those things; they have fun and go play. Children are innocent. Don't you remember the innocent days when you weren't worried about nuclear war, hurricanes, or terrorists, and you didn't know what was meant by sex in the oval office?

Childlikeness is essential to a normal human being. People need diversions where they don't have to worry about the stresses of life. There is something wonderful about husbands and wives who recognize the childlike personality in their spouse at the appropriate time.

Your husband doesn't want you to walk into his office and say, "My, my, my. It looks like a mess. I'm going to just tidy up in here." He'll drop a bomb. Professionally, you should not mother him. Personally, you should indulge his childish, boyhood personality.

Idea #5:
Wisely choose the times you want to communicate important matters.

When communicating with a man, timing is everything. Women can get men to do anything, but they have to ask at the right time. Adam damned the world to Hell by eating forbidden fruit for his wife; that is the best proof that a woman could get a man to do anything. The sooner you learn that there is timing in all that your husband does, the easier you will get along with him.

Some men mentally arrive at home about one hour after they physically arrive. (In the companion book, I'm going to address that problem.) He still has work on his mind. Whatever stressed him out on the job is weighing heavily on him. If your husband had a stressful day at work, the moment he walks in the door is not the time to drop hints about what he hasn't fixed around the house. He will wonder why he bothered coming home.

The best time to mention that something needs fixing is after he finishes a nice meal, after he cleans up a little bit, after he has his favorite pair of blue jeans on, and after he is relaxing around the house. You should cuddle up to him or sit on his lap and say, "Hey, big boy, want to do something fun like painting the room?"

It is amazing how your husband will say, "Where are the paint brushes?"

On the other hand, if you use the wrong timing, you get a lecture. He might yell at you, immaturely storm out of the house, and go hunting with his friends. So timing is really a major factor when talking to men.

IDEA #6
Broaden your interests.

Since men do something and then they have feelings about it, you should broaden your interests so that you can do things with your husband. There needs to be less combativeness and a better understanding of what a man likes to do. I am not putting the burden simply on you; I am just trying to help you understand your husband so that you can speak to him in his language. If your husband likes football, then learn about football.

Get a book on the game and learn the object and rules. There are a slew of books at Barnes and Noble and the library that will teach you how to understand football, baseball, or other non-sports activities.

You will not change him. You are not going to stop him from liking whatever he has liked since he was a little boy. If he has always been a Detroit Tigers fan, then you shouldn't say, "We don't do baseball in our house."

"Deep-seated preferences cannot be argued about."

— Oliver Wendell Holmes

If you won't let things that he likes into your house, then he might not want to be a part of your house. Sure, he might stay with you out of Christian character and decency, but it is foolish to demand what he can and cannot have or do. Don't fight his likes; broaden your interests and enjoy. That goes both ways in the marriage, and the companion book addresses the same issue to your husband.

The classic standoff between a husband and a wife occurs when the wife is trying to vacuum under her husband's feet while he is watching television. She is griping, and he just keeps punching the volume up louder. She purposefully stands in the way of the picture, and she knows that he can't see through her or around her.

No one is winning a battle there. The wife should join him or leave him alone. Good wives recognize that there are certain things her husband is going to like, and she lets him enjoy them.

COMPLAINTS	
What She Hears in Wife	*What he says in Husband*
"I can't hear the game over the vacuum cleaner; nor can I see the screen through you."	"You should take a break; you are working too hard."

Idea #7:
Write things down for your husband.

Have you ever watched an athlete interviewed after a game? When asked how he shot the winning basket, he usually answers with a jumbled answer that makes no sense. That's how men are; they communicate on a guttural level. If you don't believe that, then you don't have a teenage boy. Teenage boys tend to grunt and mumble. When I walk by the teenage boys of our church and say hello to them, I'm lucky if I get a head nod and a groan in response.

When athletes have a great play, they don't congratulate each other with words. Athletes give high-fives, pats on the rear end, and chest bumps. They are symbolically demonstrating their excitement.

Men communicate, but they tend to do it in symbolic terms; they are inferior to women in their speech skills. Men show love symbolically. Thus, they really don't like to have a heart-felt, touchy-feely talk. Men want to come home and smooch and kiss. When you want your husband to accomplish some tasks, you should write him a list with short sentences. Your husband would rather respond to written communications than verbal communications. Don't jump to the conclusion that I am stereotyping men as Neanderthals; after all, I am one of them. However, that is where men live.

"People should talk less and draw more. Personally, I would like to renounce speech altogether and, like organic nature, communicate everything I have to say visually."

– Johann Wolfgang von Goethe

Men don't like long verbal explanations of why the lawn needs to be mowed. The biggest explanation that a man needs for mowing the lawn is that you will have some cold iced tea waiting for him as he works. A cold, refreshing drink from you is reason enough for your husband to mow the lawn. He will accomplish things quicker if you use symbolic language that arouses. If you wrap your arms around him and lay a French kiss on him, he is more likely to say, "Is there more of this later?"

You should respond, "There is a whole lot more when you are done with the lawn." You will never see the lawn done so fast in your life.

Pictures really are worth a thousand words when it comes to a man. Skip the thousand words and give him a picture. Men are symbolic.

"It isn't that they can't see the solution. It's that they can't see the problem."

– G. K. Chesterton

Idea #8:
Understand that your husband takes you literally.

Men take what women say literally, but women tend to talk figuratively. Herein is a basic translational problem between the languages of Husband and Wife. I'm not asking you to change your nature as a woman, but I am asking you to understand the perspective of your husband. Men live in a contractual business world where they have to sign their name on a dotted line. A man goes home and hears his wife say, "If you do that again, I am leaving."

The man believes it; the woman didn't mean it. What the woman really meant was if you do that again and again and again and again and again and again and again and again and again and again, I am going to think about thinking about going to the other room for a few minutes.

A husband has a hard time understanding why you said something if you didn't mean it. You did mean it the moment the words went through your brain. By the time it hit your lips, you were already on another thought that was totally unrelated. One reason that men don't like to go for counsel is that women can repeatedly use counseling as a threat.

A wife can threaten, "If you don't go for counseling, then I am going to my mother's house."

The husband might well reply, "Can you go on Monday night while the football game is on so I can have the television by myself?"

To a man, that is a logical thought; to a woman, it is insensitive. Both genders need to interpret the other's communications, so it is helpful to understand how your husband interprets your words.

Idea #9:

Encourage your husband in the areas where he finds security.

A man finds security in three areas:
1. His performance at work
2. His relationship with his father

3. Acceptance and appreciation of his masculine desires for physical love

Men love to be acknowledged for being good at their work. A wise wife will acknowledge this and look for ways to encourage him. A dad and a son have a tight bond. When a man feels that you disallow his being close to his father, he feels that you are denying him a basic right of life. The wise wife will not interfere with the father and son relationship whether her husband is the father or the son. If your father-in-law is cranky or odd or strange, just write off the conflict and say, "If my husband likes his dad, then I'm okay with it." If you drive a wedge into the relationship, then your husband needs to be a very good Christian or a strong man to tolerate what he feels is an injustice.

The wise wife will get away from man bashing. Our world jokes a lot about masculinity and degrades it through humor. Women denigrate men for their sexual desires in our world. Don't do that to your husband. Don't belittle your husband if he wants sex or he wants to fool around or wants to touch or hug or kiss. The rejection will lead a weak man into pornography or an affair due to pure frustration and anger; a good man will just remain frustrated. Your husband cannot understand why you do not appreciate that he is a masculine, robust, healthy individual. Every time you push his desires aside and say, "I am so tired of you; all you talk about is sex, sex, sex," it is the equivalent of his saying, "All you talk about is cooking, or cleaning, or your emotions, or communication, or clothing, or all that junk of life."

A husband feels he has no appreciation if his wife does not recognize his ability to work, recognize the relationship with his father or his son, or acknowledge his sexual drive. When he sees women outperforming him, he wonders where he fits in this life. Men are very confused in American society. Women want to muscle in on manhood. They want to spike a ball harder than the man. There was a big to-do when the first woman in college basketball dunked during a game. I don't care; she is one more lady that I would not date if she were the only woman in the world. No hairy-legged man is interested in having a woman who outperforms him.

Chapter Four

The Basic Needs of Your Husband:
A Wife Who Respects His Masculinity

When I read a passage like I Corinthians 7:1-5, I get the impression that the Bible addresses marriage in such a vulgar level. When I say *vulgar*, I don't mean that it is immoral; I mean that it is common or on a basic level. The Bible clearly states in the passage that a reason for marriage could be to avoid fornication. It seems to say that if you cannot control yourself sexually, then you should get married. Unfortunately, this is the level where I find many of the married couples with whom I counsel.

If I ask a typical man where his marriage is at, he would typically reply, "It is okay. I don't have much to complain about. We are intimate once or twice a week. I should be happy with it."

The Apostle Paul addressed this sexual issue in the city of Corinth where fornication was rampant. The new converts were still dealing in their incest, sodomy, homosexuality, and cohabitation of men and women before marriage. Paul instructed that it was better for them to marry and fulfill their sexual desires in that marriage relationship than to continue in their lasciviousness. Marriage was offered as a cure for those sins.

Marriage became crude in Corinth, and it still is in the twenty-first century. Too many people today get married for the same reason they got married in those days—convenience. People marry for financial convenience, a tax break, and children, or because they are lonely or sexually starved and want to fulfill their lust.

Many marriages have occurred because a couple conceived after sleeping together ten or a hundred times. They had lots of sex, but it got old, and they only got married because it was the right and convenient thing to do since their child would be born. The marriage is obligatory, and most of these couples would be fortunate to have an average marriage.

Marriage has become ordinary. There is so much more to marriage than what is contained in the average union. Building a good marriage takes an incredible amount of work. Couples marry and still don't know today why they got married. They never figured out their roles, and they started off on the wrong foot.

The modern answer to that problem is to get

divorced and start all over again. People then start sleeping around again, jump the gun on marriage, and never break the repetitious errors that have resulted in a plethora of messed-up people. Marriage has been demeaned, and its sacredness has been shredded.

Your husband might think of sex as his greatest need, but it ultimately is not his greatest need. If sex is a husband's greatest need, then he is grasping at the straws of his masculinity. The action makes him feel manly. When a man feels that sex is his greatest need, he is likely not feeling masculine in other areas of his life. This chapter addresses what every man needs from his wife. The wise wife will consider these ideas and implement them into her marriage.

Your husband does not understand what types of protection you need. He does not automatically know what you need physically, mentally, emotionally, or spiritually. When you assume that he does, you are not respecting that he is a man. Your husband wants to provide these protections, but they are not innate.

Tell your husband how he can protect you. Many ladies in my counseling sessions tell me, "My husband doesn't understand what I need as a woman." Ninety percent of all men are clueless to the needs of a woman. Your husband doesn't ponder the depths nor the surface of your emotional and spiritual needs.

Your husband will not mind if you say, "I need something, and I need a big, strong, strapping, wonderful, fantastic, big-bulging-muscled, bright-eyed hunk to help me with it."

Most men will say, "That's me. You are talking about me, aren't you?"

If you explain to your husband what you need, like, or desire, it is amazing how quickly you will get it. A man understands when you say, "I need this," but does not understand what you want when you say, "You never do this for me." For instance, if you want your husband to pick up his clothes instead of leaving them around, you should say, "I need your help in picking up your clothes." Your husband will understand that. You should not say, "You never pick up your clothes!" You are implying that he needs to pick them up, but you are not respecting his manhood; he'll probably throw more clothes on the floor.

Men do not respond to a woman's accusatory tone or attitude. When a man is accused, it is an insult to his manhood. A man doesn't want to admit to himself, "I think I should have done that already," when a woman belittles him.

For an example, allow me to use the old chivalrous idea that a man is supposed to open a car door for a lady. I still do that for my wife. She is a lady, so I want to do that for her.

The Basic Needs of Your Husband... | 71

Suppose your husband doesn't open the door for you. He jumps in the car and yells, "Get in!"

What you don't want to say is, "I thought I was married to a man." With that statement a man will start the car, slam it in reverse, and take off. He doesn't want his manhood put on a frying pan and burned.

What you do want to say is, "I married this incredible, phenomenal and amazing man. Once in a while he is so focused on his mission and his grandeur and his greatness that even he occasionally forgets poor little old me and how helpless I am. I need that big, strong boy to come help me open my door."

Halfway through your statement, he will start thinking that you are looking to make trouble. However, if he has any masculinity, he will get out of the car and come open your door. You can use his masculinity in your favor by asking him to display it.

"The only difference between stumbling blocks and stepping stones is the way in which we use them."

– Adrianna Doyle

If you want to take it a step further, you should put sexual buzz into your words. Give him the look that says, "I'll make it up to you tonight," or make a suggestive statement like, "This is great foreplay." Men always understand when women put a slightly sexual spin on words. Your husband will appreciate a slightly naughty wife. Your husband will understand that you need him to come open the door or whatever else you want him to do for your protection.

Don't be financially independent of your husband. If you are really good with your money, don't remind your husband that you don't need him financially, especially in the heat of the battle. Couples who have lived together without getting married have that philosophy. The woman has to provide for herself because the man might leave one day when there are no strings attached. That philosophy has permeated throughout our society and into godly marriages.

If you earn money, don't remind your husband that you will get along without him. What you are saying to your husband is, "I measure your manhood everyday. If you get a failing grade, then I'm leaving." A man does not need to be reminded how unnecessary he is; a man wants to feel that he is necessary.

Society has portrayed men as buffoons on television and radio programs and in commercials. Men are looked at as stupid and in need of the wife to bail them out of trouble. It has become easy for men to feel unnecessary in our culture.

Truthfully, a wife needs her husband. You might have gotten married only because he was handsome or

The Basic Needs of Your Husband... | 73

offered an escape from your parents' house, but you have grown dependent on him and still need whatever protection he provides. It would not hurt your marriage to let your husband know that you need him. One way you disrespect him is when you say, "I have my own checkbook, and I have my own money, so I don't need you."

Men love to rise to the occasion; they like to come through. They want to be a clutch player and have a reputation of reliability. Your marital love is killed when you develop self-sufficiency from your husband.

Don't have more confidence in outside leadership than you do in your husband. Don't be more loyal to your boss than you are to your husband. I think you should be loyal to your boss, but you ultimately should be loyal to your husband. Don't talk too much about how wonderful or smart or wise any other man is in front of your husband. Your husband does not want to hear about the greatness of another man from your lips.

Be careful if you have a job. Be respectful and loyal to your co-workers. Always be courteous, polite, loyal, and respectful to the boss. Whether your boss or some co-worker is handsome or ugly, fat or skinny, or athletic or pathetic, you should be careful about how you talk about him around your husband. He doesn't care if the guy is brilliant, creative, phenomenal, skilled, talented, or a great leader. Your husband cares that you think he, not the other guy, is great and that he provides security for you.

Don't resist your husband's physical affection. This unspoken, unpardonable sin is the number one way to crush your husband's spirit. Sexual rejection is the ultimate putdown. Your husband knows what it means when you just slightly move away from his lips when he tries to kiss you. Your husband can interpret your defensive posturing when he embraces you. He understands the I-am-really-busy look. All of it breaks down his masculinity.

Ladies get dolled up with make-up, and then they don't want their husband to kiss it off. Your husband likes it when you look sexy, but then you get afraid that he will mess up your make-up. Men wonder why women get all dressed up. Is it so that your husband can't touch you because you want to be a museum display? If you are trying to look sexy, your husband is going to want sex, and that is not going to do wonders for your lipstick or hair.

When you resist physical affection, it is the unspoken crushing of a man's spirit. Rejection of appetites is crushing. Don't use sex as a weapon. The Bible makes it very clear that your bodies belong to one another. *"The wife hath not power of her own body, but the husband: and likewise also the husband hath not power of his own body, but the wife."* (I Corinthians 7:4)

The Basic Needs of Your Husband... | 75

A popular statement that I hear from husbands and wives during counseling is, "I know what the Bible says, but...." When you throw out the Bible, you are throwing out principles, and those principles strengthen your marriage.

When people will not follow procedural policies (as the Bible contains), they will begin to break moral policies. Your home must have some core rules that it follows. You cannot have moments of hot-headedness where you blow off some steam and say, "Well, that is just the way I see it." If that is your argument, then your husband has a right to have his own way of seeing it. If you are going to be a blockhead, then your husband has the right to be a blockhead. Have some wisdom in your home. Two brick walls built up against each other will not solve the problems in your marriage.

Your husband might be taking physical advantage of you and abusing you. I am not talking about not resisting that type of physical attention. The Bible doesn't say that a wife has to be abused. The answer to the abuse problem is 9-1-1.

A physically abused wife will be amazed at how much her husband's attitude changes when he is in handcuffs. Women don't have to turn to divorce lawyers. A divorce lawyer can't keep a husband from hitting his wife. The policeman and the judge can stop that. No matter how much a husband doesn't like a wife, he will stop hitting her if he spends enough time in jail. This whole method is heavy-handed, but I prefer to see a wife to first try the following Biblical approach.

A wife has a powerful guard against her husband's abuse. According to the Bible, she is the weaker vessel, and God affords her His protection. *"Likewise, ye wives, be in subjection to your own husbands; that, if any obey not the word, they also may without the word be won by the conversation of the wives; While they behold your chaste conversation coupled with fear."* (I Peter 3:1-2)

The protection that God affords is your godly lifestyle. A holy and godly woman is what captures a man's masculinity. A mouthy, sassy, loud woman challenges a man's masculinity because she is right in his face. When a woman escalates her volume and words, the softest and kindest of men can get very nasty. I Peter 3:4 teaches that a wife should have a "meek and quiet spirit." This means that you must be able to calm down and not provoke your husband's anger.

CHAPTER FIVE

The Basic Needs of Your Husband:

A Wife Who Respects Him and Believes in Him as a Leader

Few things are as absent in America as strong leadership. Nowhere is that leadership as lacking as in the home. Little boys will turn into incredible leaders if mom and dad have their act together; otherwise, they are going to turn into very poor leaders. One of the critical periods in a man's leadership is the transition from living with his parents to living with his wife.

Reinforce to your husband that he has authority from God to be the leader in the home. I Corinthians 11:3 says, *"But I would have you know, that the head of every man is Christ; and the head of the woman is the man; and the head of Christ is God."* Ephesians 5:23 says, *"For the husband is the head of the wife, even as Christ is the head of the church: and he is the saviour of the body."* These verses aren't culturally popular, but I believe that God's ways are the best ways. A wife's submission qualifies her husband for church leadership. Many good men never lead in a church because their wives have never convinced them that they are good leaders. I Timothy 3:5 says, *"...For if a man know not how to rule his own house, how shall he take care of the church of God?"* If you won't submit to your husband, God says that nobody else will either.

Impart confidence to your husband. If your husband wants to be a deacon or Sunday school teacher, or if he wants to go for a promotion at work, then believe in him. Reassure him that his position of leadership comes from God. Because a man is created in the image of God, he wants to believe that his position is God's will. If you don't reassure him of that, then you destroy his confidence.

Many men across America are grievously afflicted by emotions because they wanted to go to the mission field or work in an American ministry, but their wife would not submit to the idea. Whether it is in the spiritual or secular arena, don't be the one who cuts off your husband's leadership. Let him come to his own conclusion that he can't do something. Let him flunk out of Bible college or let the boss tell him that he is not that good. Don't be the one who plays God in his life.

Support your husband's decisions because God works through a man's decisions whether they are

The Basic Needs of Your Husband... | 79

good or bad. That is hard to swallow, but it is true. A bad decision might have been God's will to teach you and your husband a lesson.

The Magna Charta is one of the greatest documents of humanity other than the Word of God. The Magna Charta said that people would be ruled by law and not by men. The Magna Charta was the foundational underpinnings of our United States Constitution. Men don't rule other men: laws rule men. Men are elected to create the laws that the people decide they should follow. That is one reason why America has lasted as long as it has and been the envy of every other nation in the world.

My church operates under the same principle. Procedures and policies govern my church, and that keeps strong personalities from overrunning it. People in my church are always clashing, and they will clash until the Lord returns. Problems are always solved by following the rules that we have established; when we follow the rules, the problems always seem to take care of themselves.

Marriage is similar. The wife should not decide to override her husband's decision. You may believe that your husband made a wrong decision, but did you really think that you married a man that is infallible and incapable of making a wrong decision?

Leaders make mistakes. They pull the trigger. They have been empowered to decide, and they live with the repercussions of their decision. Good people need to understand that even bad decisions by God-given authority can be used by God to ultimately make things work out right.

You must accept that your husband will make bad decisions. Bad decisions reveal a man's needs and allow the wife to appeal and demonstrate godly character. You cope with the bad decision by explaining to your husband that God is using him to benefit your spiritual life.

Don't tell your husband that he made a stupid decision; he already knows that. He needs a wife that says, "I am on your team. Good or bad, right or wrong, you are the man God put in charge. I believe God uses even what you call your mistakes to better our station in life and to work through us and teach us spiritual truths." No man would be upset by that statement because it is pure, wonderful, and godly.

If you don't understand that, then you will take matters into your own hands and make all of the same mistakes that are mentioned in this book. Your husband doesn't need to be put in his place. The marriage would not be better if it were run by you because God did not give you that authority.

There are powers that are not given to me in this

life, and I don't worry about not having those powers. As a man, it does not insult me that I am not the President of the United States. My inability to achieve that position does not diminish me or put me down. Instead, it reminds me that God has picked out one person who is accountable for the country. If the President makes a bad decision, we can still survive as a country because God put him in charge.

Don't use your attitude to resist your husband's decisions. Many wives are good at not verbalizing their protests yet just as good at showing their displeasure through their attitude. When your negative attitudes are translated into Husband, you might as well say outright, "I don't agree with you, and I don't believe in you." Your spirit and heart show through your attitudes, your tones, and your facial expressions. Wives have a lot of power to nibble at a man's masculinity. You can make your husband feel like a blob who is in your way without outrightly expressing it.

Your spirit controls your husband's ambitions. Your response is the toggle switch that says, "Go for it" or "Forget about it." A man can sense a woman's attitude as quickly as he can tell whether it is hot or cold outside.

Avoid reminding your husband of the poor decisions he has made throughout your marriage. You will destroy your husband's manhood. Couples who have been married ten or more years need to have an occasional time where they draw a line in the sand and decide to start over. They need to put past mistakes behind them and go on. Every so many years you need to commit to not digging up past mistakes. Each year you and your husband will make new mistakes. Husbands don't remember as well as wives do. A man's mind can't compete with the past problems because he often doesn't remember them.

When you bring up past failures, your husband will wonder if you have any appreciation for his past successes. He wants to say, "If I'm such a failure, then why don't you get out of the house that I have paid for, and give me the keys to the cars that I have paid for, and give me back the clothes I have purchased for you, and get out."

"Few things help an individual more than to place responsibility upon him, and to let him know that you trust him."

– Booker T. Washington

The logic of a man is different from a woman's logic. Reviewing his past failures and showing an attitude of disagreement is a challenge to your husband's masculinity.

Don't take matters into your own hands. Don't become your husband's conscience; you don't have to make decisions for him. Demand of yourself that you will let your husband make the decision.

The norms of our society dictate that a man should automatically assume that his mother makes the choices. At work, policy decides choices. Men love making decisions, but our world is taking choices away from men.

I have a suggestion for the next time your husband says, "Where do you want to go for dinner?"

Tell him, "I married a man, and I am so proud of myself for doing it. I am so proud of you because you are a man, and I will not be your mother; I will not be your child. I am your sweetheart. You swept me off my feet, and I told you I would go with you whether good or bad, right or wrong, sick or healthy, poor or rich. Take me where you want to go. I don't care if it is a picnic in the woods, McDonald's, or downtown Chicago. You pick because you are the man."

Don't put your husband down. Exalt his manhood and let him wrestle with it a little bit. If you argue about decisions, you will put your husband down. You can train your husband to jump through hoops, but when he is done being trained, he will no longer be a man. You might need a man sometime; they come in handy during a crisis.

When a wife intrudes into one responsibility, her husband often surrenders other responsibilities as well. Proverbs 14:1 says, *"Every wise woman buildeth her house: but the foolish plucketh it down with her hands."* Here is a

84 | How to Speak Husband

typical scenario that I see during counseling sessions.

The wife says, "I can't get my husband to lead."

I ask, "What decisions do you let him make?"

"He doesn't make any decisions," she replies.

I then ask, "So what do you do then?"

The wife replies, "I make them for him."

I always tell them, "That is the problem."

"If I don't make them, we don't get anything done," she argues.

At that point, I teach a wife what I mentioned a few paragraphs ago. You can use your femininity to get your husband to lead. There is a way to speak your husband's language that he cannot resist. If you properly speak to him in Husband instead of Wife, you can cross over the threshold of many problems. Unfortunately, instead of using your femininity as a woman, you resort to the masculine trait of leading. If your husband wanted your masculinity, he would have married a man instead.

When you start making the decisions, your husband will start to assume that he is just the paycheck around the house. He will build a wall of silence because he doesn't want to fuss. Ultimately, he will let you lead the house because you have walked into his area of responsibility and he doesn't want to compete with a woman.

Development of leadership abilities in your husband and your son has been stymied because they

have grown up in a woman-dominated society. Men have learned a new place in life during the past 25 years or so. Boys are having a harder and harder time developing a character of decisiveness. Because of that, men today get married ten years later than they did 50 years ago and seven years later than they did 25 years ago.

You may think that your teenage boy is hard to control, but he is supposed to be hard to control. Boys go through a stage where they try to express leadership. They will make a lot of wrong choices because they lack wisdom. Parents require a lot of shock absorption to allow their boy to make decisions without remaking them for him.

Parents want to re-grab the reins of a boy's life, but they destroy his decision-making development. The decisions he makes might mess up the bumper of the car, ruin expensive tools, or break windows. Parents don't want their boys to make mistakes at home, but the consequence is that the boy makes his mistakes by getting a girl pregnant or hitting someone with his car while he is drunk. Parents have to expect foolishness from their teenage boys. Instead, they avoid the foolishness, but develop a man who can't make decisions. They develop a husband who will have a frustrated wife because he won't make decisions.

Your husband may have been brought up in a

woman-dominated home and society. You have to encourage him to make the decisions. The next time he asks you where you would like to go out and eat, you should reply, "I love it when you make the decisions." Encourage your husband to be a man, and you will be happier as a feminine wife.

Your husband needs a loyal wife. Your husband needs your loyalty when a mistake is made and pressure is increased. Loyalty can only be demonstrated in adversity; thus, problems can be good for a marriage. A demonstration of loyalty is impossible when you are in agreement with your husband. If you follow your husband because you agree with him, then you are exhibiting common sense and have not had the opportunity to exhibit loyalty. Loyalty to your husband is hard because it means that when you do not think he is right, you still believe that he is your God-given authority.

When you struggle with a decision by your husband, here are questions to ask yourself:
1. Is my husband appointed by God to be the leader of our home?
2. Do I disagree with his decision because from my vantage point I see it differently?
3. Do I disagree because his decision is immoral?
4. Do I disagree with my husband because I am trying to protect him like a mother would?

5. Do I disagree because I am embarrassed for my husband to make a mistake?
6. Do I disagree because I just know I am right and he should listen to me?
7. Do I disagree because it is hard for me to humble myself and be loyal?

These are all tough questions with which you must wrestle. If there is an immoral decision he is making, then you might need help from a pastor. However, unless the marriage is fractured and broken, you should never ask others for counsel without your husband's approval.

The other questions are ultimately answered by your attitude of submission. This is where the rubber meets the road. These are questions you should have answered before you got married. These are topics that you and your husband need to discuss and iron out.

Your husband needs admiration for his leadership. Your husband needs your praise. Let your husband hear you praise him to other people. You would remove doubts from your husband's confidence if he heard you talk well of him to someone else. Your husband wants you to give him attention. When your husband is talking to others, look at him admiringly. Let other people think that you think that what he says is important. Believe it or not, they will start thinking that what your husband says is important.

Your husband needs you to encourage him not to give up. Encourage your husband to express his deepest wishes and then encourage him to accomplish those. Your husband needs you to have patience in times of pressure as he does chase down his dream. Don't add to the pressure when your husband is going through a brutal time of pressure at work. Don't add to the pressure by saying, "I know you've got pressure at work, but what about me?" You are adding pressure instead of relieving it.

Your husband needs you to have enthusiasm for his achievements. When you reject your husband's achievements, you are rejecting him. Sharing his excitement is more important to him than sharing his work. One reason your husband married you was to share his spirit. When you don't share his spirit and his excitement, he feels you reject him. A man's work is his life. A man enjoys compliments from his co-workers, but it is more important for him to hear his wife say, "Well done."

Please don't act like it is a pain to be married to your husband. It is not an interference with your life. Treat him as what he is; he is God's man for your world and for your life.

Chapter Six

The Basic Needs of Your Husband:

A Wife Who Will Continue to Develop Inward and Outward Beauty

I would like to teach wives how to become the woman of their husband's dreams. What wife wouldn't want to be that? If your husband looked at another woman, you would be filled with jealousy and rage. My guess is that your husband doesn't even think about how you could become the woman of his dreams, but don't you want to be? I am not going to give you what men who lust after pornography want in the ideal woman. From a Biblical perspective, allow me to suggest how you could become that woman for your husband.

Start with your hair and dress style. I Corinthians 11:10 says, *"For this cause ought the woman to have power on her head because of the angels."* That is a strange verse, isn't it? Hair is symbolic; it is the symbol of being under authority. How a woman wears her hair or how she expresses herself through her hair is a statement of who she believes is her authority. You should ask your husband how he would like you to wear your hair, and by all means do what he prefers.

I Corinthians 11:15 says, *"But if a woman have long hair, it is a glory to her: for her hair is given her for a covering."* God teaches that a woman's hair is given to her for a covering. This covering is not a covering of modesty; it is a covering of her authority. Your hair says that you are under the authority of your husband. Every husband wants a wife who would admit that she is under his God-given authority. A woman's hair seems to be a basis for spiritual protection. A woman wears her hair longer than a man for spiritual protection. Hair is a woman's glory. It is a glorious thing to be married to a man who is your leader.

Ephesians 5:24 says, *"Therefore as the church is subject unto Christ, so let the wives be to their own husbands in every thing."* Your hairstyle should reflect your husband's wishes. When you spend extra time and effort on your appearance, you are expressing your respect for your husband.

A large gripe of men is that women spend an inordinate amount of time getting ready. Women complain that men complain about it. Your husband should not complain because you are taking time to prepare yourself because you respect him. That is why you do it, isn't it? Your husband should notice the time you put in to making yourself look nice. I will address that issue for you in the companion book.

Unfortunately, we have been raised to believe that we should always tell a woman that she looks wonderful even if we don't believe it. That's a product of the women's-rights movement and not of Biblical teaching.

The failure of women to understand their scriptural role has damaged our country. Defying your husband's wishes on how you look hurts your marriage. Women tend to dress for other women, and not for their man. Women want other women to be impressed with how they dress. Women wear their hair either for their convenience or so that other women can appreciate their faddish, trendy styles. Very few women ever say to their husband, "Tell me how you like my hair," and then they wear it the way their husband suggests.

Rarely will a woman say, "My husband wants me to wear my hair this way," when she is complimented or confronted by another woman about her hairstyle. Women wear their hair the way they want to and ignore the Biblical teaching. Hair is a symbol of your respect and your submission to your husband. When you take away the symbol of respect and submission, it is because there is no respect and submission in your heart.

I hope you are not a wife who finds it hard to be submissive and to live with a man who expresses his views. Unfortunately, a submissive wife is a rare find. I doubt if I know more than ten women who are Biblically submissive to their husbands. I know many good Christian women who do very noble works and who are very good Christians that love the Lord. They would do anything that the church asked. However, they aren't submissive. God will not predominately judge a wife for her works in the church; He will judge her for her works in her marriage.

The Scriptures teach that a husband should have a wife who says, "Tell me how you want me to dress. Tell me how you want me to wear my hair. Tell me how you want me to behave. Tell me what your desires are." Those are hard things to request, but God says these things are attached to the heart symbolically; they are not attached just to the outward styles. Your hair and dress are not a matter of fashion, trend, or style; they are a statement of who your authority is.

This battle goes back to the Garden of Eden. Man felt usurped when the woman took advantage of him. Adam was not deceived like Eve, but he took of the fruit for the sake of his wife. He knew it would damn his soul and bring corruption to all of society. Since then, there has been a power play between men and women. Some women want to insist that they know what is best and right and will adopt whatever styles they choose. These women want to run the home, and their men don't stand up to them because they want peace.

Years ago I told my wife that I would run our home. I told her that I would fight with her over it. Someday I will not answer to her, but I will answer to God for how I ran my home. God empowered me with that authority, and with it came great responsibility.

Authority issues must be settled in every home. Many men would sleep on the couch if they went home and declared that they were making some decisions. Despite the world's plan for running a home, you would realize your ultimate happiness as a wife if you would organize your marriage according to God's plan.

Care of your home is a symbol of your gratefulness to your husband. Every man wants a woman who is grateful for his provision. How a lady takes care of the home is a symbol of the husband's wisdom, provision, and protection. Care of your home is not restricted to cleaning up dirt and clutter; it is also in how you care for the items within the home.

A wife's spirit sets the atmosphere in the home. Keep your home free of clutter. Men don't mind if the kids are playing with toys, but when a man has to walk through a junkyard to get into his bedroom, it offends his spirit. He might even be the one who contributes to the junk, but a wife needs to keep it free of clutter. Provide good music in your home that produces a cozy atmosphere. Your home ought to be a very happy place both in sound and in sight and in smell.

Watch your weight. Your weight is a symbol of your husband's leadership and of your self control. Proverbs 23:21 tells us God is concerned about overeating and being overweight. Physical or spiritual concerns can cause you to be overweight, and it would be wise to address either issue. Romans 12:1 says that we are to dedicate our bodies as a living sacrifice to God. We should be careful not to consume the wrong foods at the wrong times, and we should take care of medical issues that plague our bodies.

Develop a meek and quiet spirit. I Peter 3:4 teaches that a woman should have this kind of spirit. Meekness is yielding one's rights. A quiet spirit is conquering fear and worry. Women need to control being hyper and over-emotional. Our society says that it is the norm for a woman to be out of control emotionally, but the Bible says the opposite. The woman is supposed to be the one in the home who has emotional stability.

Menstrual cycles and menopause don't make any woman out of sorts; they magnify what she is already. If you are an undisciplined person, the menstrual cycle and menopause will magnify that a hundredfold, and people will see what you truly are in your heart. These natural processes have become another excuse to hide behind. We can blame God for it. We can blame Eve for it. We can blame Sarah, Abraham, Noah, or anyone else, but the bottom line is that God didn't give those things to women as an excuse for wild behavior. God says that the woman is supposed to be quiet in her spirit; she should be free from erratic behavior.

Some women should consider taking off a day or two or three from work during their menstrual cycle. Some need to sleep more, and some need to take medication. The cycle does not give a wife the right to bite off her husband's head and yell at her kids any more than a husband has the right to flip out if he is not feeling well.

Did you know that if you have terrible menstrual cramps, you should check your health? That problem can be caused by horrible health and eating problems. If that is your problem, do you have a poor diet? Do you exercise? When people let themselves go physically, their health problems are magnified exponentially. I've heard ladies blame God because He gave them a menstrual cycle each month. Thus, they reason that it is God's fault that a wife bites her husband's head off while yelling and cursing.

Decide ahead of time how you will behave during this time. Reaction is irresponsibility; you can't blame it on personal weakness. You do not have to behave that way; the Bible is contrary to that behavior. The Bible says to develop a meek and quiet spirit.

Display the poise that shows you are in control of your external surroundings. Poise is a symbol of a husband's training. The basic element of poise is contentment; ladies with poise are appropriate. Women who are appropriate have a basic contentment which comes from self-acceptance. Biblical self-acceptance is seeing that God has made you the way you are. Of course, we contribute to some of our problems, but being well-groomed keeps you from being self-conscious.

You should dress sharply so that you do not have to think about your clothing the rest of the day. It is easy to become self-conscious when you don't match. You don't appear to have poise when you are always tugging your skirt down so that it is long enough. You don't have poise if you are always pulling up your top to avoid showing cleavage. Buy appropriate clothing; it is better than walking around with an outfit that makes you self-conscious. When you take away your poise, you look as though you do not fit into your husband's surroundings. He wants a woman who looks like she fits alongside of him.

Chapter Seven

The Basic Needs of Your Husband:

A Wife Who Can Lovingly Appeal to Him When He Is Wrong and Can Wisely Respond to Those Who Question Him

What does a wife do when she knows her husband has stepped outside the boundaries of his role? This is a critical question because a husband and wife are a team. Your husband has the authority in your marriage, but it does not mean he is exempt from committing mistakes. When a husband steps outside of his God-given boundaries, a godly wife must use every available scriptural resource to keep her husband from bringing damage and reproach to the cause of Christ and to himself.

If you are concerned that his mistakes are a poor reflection on you, then you are missing the point of being a wife. This is evidenced by a wife's loud mouth, insults, and motherly patronizing. You are not his mother, but you are responsible for him. When your husband makes mistakes, you must be careful to speak in Husband so that your words in Wife do not crush his spirit.

You have a right to appeal to your husband. There are several examples in the Bible of people who have gone to God and asked Him to rethink and change a decision. If sinful humans are allowed to appeal to a holy God, then a wife can definitely appeal to her sinful husband. If you do not learn how to appeal to God, then you will never learn how to appeal to your husband because your husband is made in the image of God. Your husband can be less inclined to agree with you than God would because he has pride, sin, and arrogance. A proper appeal will increase the respect and love from your husband because of what you have done.

Men do not want to be fools, and you should keep your husband from looking like one. You can easily embarrass your husband by straightening his tie or picking lint off of his suit. Public arenas are not the places to correct your husband or your children.

The proper way to appeal to God is not to seek to change God. Rather, you must appeal to God on behalf of His reputation. When God was going to destroy Sodom, Abraham appealed to God. Abraham said to God, *"Shall not the Judge of all the earth do right?"* Abraham appealed to God's position and His sense of fairness, justice, and godliness. For instance, Moses argued with God about destroying the Israelites. God said to Moses in Exodus 32:9, 10, *"...I have seen this people, and, behold, it is a stiffnecked people: Now therefore let me alone, that my wrath may wax hot against them, and that I may consume them: and I will make of thee a great nation."*

Moses replied in Exodus 32:11-13, *"...LORD, why doth thy wrath wax hot against thy people, which thou hast brought forth out of the land of Egypt with great power, and with a mighty hand? Wherefore should the Egyptians speak, and say, For mischief did he bring them out, to slay them in the mountains, and to consume them from the face of the earth? Turn from thy fierce wrath, and repent of this evil against thy people. Remember Abraham, Isaac, and Israel, thy servants, to whom thou swarest by thine own self, and saidst unto them, I will multiply your seed as the stars of heaven, and all this land that I have spoken of will I give unto your seed, and they shall inherit it for ever."*

Moses essentially said, "If You destroy the people, then everyone will know that You aren't keeping Your promises to people. Everyone will think that even You couldn't lead them out of the wilderness! Your reputation is at stake!"

Those stories are not in the Bible to show us that God is inept; they are there to show us how and why we can approach God. God wants you to notice how men

"Saying nothing... sometimes says the most."

– Emily Dickinson

would talk to Him about a decision with which they did not agree. You should do the same with your husband. You should approach him with the argument over his reputation. That is how you can rightfully help your husband change his mind and keep him from making poor decisions.

Chapter Eight

The Basic Needs of Your Husband:

A Wife Who Is Grateful for All He Has Done and Is Doing for Her

*H*usbands love gratitude. Nothing destroys gratitude like having expectations. The more expectations you have of your husband and your marriage, the less gratitude you will have. Gratefulness is the basis of happiness. A happy wife is a prize for a husband. An unhappy wife is a public rebuke to a husband.

No one is more watched in my church than my wife. When I make Biblical statements that seem as though they might offend, people look to see my wife's reaction. A man who preached around the country once observed that each church with growth problems contained an unhappy pastor's wife. People watch the spirit of a wife to determine the potential of her husband.

Men are attracted to the gratefulness in a woman more than any other quality. Men are turned on by beauty and sensuality, but ultimately that is not what a man needs. Sexy women scare men because they are manipulative, and men don't like to be controlled. Godly men who are seduced by sexy women later feel angry because they feel used. Sensuality arouses a man, but he doesn't really like a woman flaunting her powers in his face; he finds it irritating.

Not all males reject an over-sensual woman, but all men do. There are males who live for sensual pleasure, but they are crude and vulgar and have lost their manhood. They have lost self-respect, and others pity the wives of such a man. Base, crude, vulgar, evil-minded, and wicked men enjoy viewing the cleavage of every woman. Your husband might have slithered into being the sensual type. If so, then he needs you to help him restore his manhood.

Happily married men enjoy the cleavage of their wife, but they don't want to see the cleavage of another woman because they don't want to be manipulated. Men are not ultimately attracted to cleavage hanging out. The eyes of men are enticed by it, but they are never satisfied because they want gratitude. There is a huge difference between the satisfaction that comes with no guilt and the satisfaction that comes with guilt. Sexy women are grateful that they can control a man; they are not grateful to the man for what he has done. Too many women in our society—even Christian women—have bought into the lie that sensuality equals femininity. Men who are righteous and holy aren't looking for that; they are looking for gratitude. A wife who doesn't understand these basic things gets jealous of other attractive women and pouts when her husband prefers that she have a happy spirit. When a wife has a happy spirit and is grateful, a man feels like he has hit a home run. What a man simply wants is a woman who is grateful that she is married to a man; this is very attractive to a man.

If your husband cuts back on what he gives you financially, it might be that he feels that you are ungrateful. He shouldn't do that because he is treating you like a child. By cutting back financially, he is trying to decrease your expectations so that you will be more likely to find him grateful. I know that doesn't make sense to you, but it does to him; I don't think it makes sense either. However, you will always be happier if you expect nothing and are genuinely grateful for each expression of your husband's love.

Your husband needs you to be content with godliness. I Timothy 6:6 says, *"But godliness with contentment is great gain."* Many Christian ladies leave out godliness while trying to be content. Godliness means that you set your affections on things above. Husbands are materially

"Flattery is the infantry of negotiation."

– Lord Chandos

minded. The Bible commands a husband to be materially minded in expressing his love for his wife. However, if a wife only sees the things that her husband possesses and purchases for her as a measure of his love, then he feels he is nothing more than an ATM.

A wife should translate the receiving of things into gratitude. A husband wants to feel gratitude for being a loving man as is evidenced by his provision. A man receives love in this way instead of just receiving new things into his home. As a wife you are supposed to set your affection on the love that is displayed by your husband's provision and not on the material object.

A wife's priorities differ from a man's priorities, and this misunderstanding leads to some problems. Men are concerned about activities and expenditures that build his reputation and provide for his wife's security. Although you don't always see the importance, your husband needs to know that you appreciate what he is doing for you. When your husband makes mistakes, could you appreciate that he hasn't made bigger catastrophic mistakes? Maybe your husband has lost a lot of money, but he has been faithful. Why not praise him for being faithful, then? He is not a stupid lug who doesn't lift his feet when you vacuum the carpet or doesn't give you enough money. Unfortunately, that's how many a husband thinks his wife feels about him. Praise your husband for that which he has done wisely.

Chapter Nine

The Basic Needs of Your Husband:

A Wife Who Will Be Praised by Other People

This need sounds strange, but the Bible talks about people praising a virtuous woman. A husband needs to know that his wife is somebody who is respected in the community of peers in which they run. A man doesn't want to think that he is married to the loser of the group because his wife doesn't contribute to the world.

Your husband wants to know that your neighbors respect you. Your husband wants to know that you are respected when he is not around. Everyone has bad days, but your husband doesn't want a wife whose presence makes others wince. Your husband wants a wife who is known by others as being a standout in some area.

Your husband needs to think that others think that

"The deepest principle of human nature is the craving to be appreciated."
– William James

he married well. Wives are the same way; they like it when their husband is praised because it looks like they married well. A praised wife is a feather in your husband's cap. If you bring deserved criticism, insults, and jokes, then your husband might think that he didn't marry very well.

Your husband needs a wife who takes pride in her health and beauty. Your husband needs to feel that he has a wife that is looking out for his name. He wants you to lift his name up to another level so that other people will think that she is married to an awesome man.

CHAPTER TEN

The Basic Needs of Your Husband:

A Wife With the Meekness to Meet His Needs

Society is wrestling with the question, "Why do we need men?" Women can have artificial insemination; they can give birth to test-tube babies. Many women in this world are out to prove that they don't need men. They have their own sports associations and even play amongst the boys' football and wrestling teams. Women can even curse better nowadays.

Men can no longer outfight women. Men in our society feel that there is not much need for them. That is why this book discussed the man's role first; we need to get back to what the Bible says. Men weren't made for ladies. Men were accomplishing their work in the Garden before the woman ever came along.

God gave you to your husband to help meet his needs. You need to realize his needs and help him fulfill them. When God gave Eve to Adam, she listened to the wrong person and damned mankind to Hell; that's not the kind of help your husband needs.

Wives like to tell their husbands what they don't like about them, and when those words are translated into Husband, they break his spirit. Too many wives don't like their husband's sex drive, masculinity, and leadership. The wife should encourage those God-given roles. The Bible is very clear about the role of a woman in church. In blunt terms the Bible says that a wife should go to church, keep quiet, and listen to her husband. Wives are trying to cram an ungodly role down their husbands' throats, and then they wonder why their men don't like going to church.

Please don't trash talk the man for which God made you. Too many women that I counsel tell me what is wrong with their husband. Wives can't understand why they don't have a happy marriage, yet they verbally trounce their husband in front of other people. Yes, your husband has many faults. However, you must be committed to him, and the two of you are going to work the problems out. Problems will work themselves out when you play your God-given roles and allow your husband to play his roles. God designed you that way, and your marriage will run a lot smoother when you speak the language of Husband.

The Basic Needs of Your Husband... | 111

If you are going to criticize your husband, this book will not be of much help to you. Yes, your husband has faults, but you must first deal with your issues and your roles and not with what you perceive are your husband's problems. You need to exalt your husband because if you do not exalt him, then you are not fulfilling the purpose for which God put you on this earth.

The companion book, *How to Speak Wife*, is as hard-hitting to your husband as this book is to you. It will help your husband understand your roles and what he can do to support them. Christian men should exalt womanhood to the highest position of any of God's creatures, even above themselves. Your husband should not be on an ego trip to prove his superiority and to prove how fortunate you were when you got to marry him.

"The easiest, the most tempting, and the least creative response to conflict within an organization is to pretend it does not exist."

– Lyle E. Schaller

Your husband wants you. Contrary to what the world says, your husband is not interested in what every woman thinks about him; he is interested in you. Why do you think he proposed to you? Perhaps that desire is off track at this particular time in your life, but the two of you need to get it back on track, and I believe that interest will be reawakened when you both assume your proper roles.

Wife, grab the problems by the horns and say to your husband, "I know you had a rough start in marriage, but I believe in you. I married you because you are going to provide security for me. I want you. I find great joy in your presence, and I believe you are the man for my life." In Husband those words impart confidence and hope.

Your husband needs to have that confidence from you to accomplish the purpose God gives to him. To the degree that you give your husband that support, you will find tremendous security and strength as a feminine and Biblical wife.

Do you have a better understanding of Wife and Husband? Do you have a better understanding of your husband's language? Do you understand that you do not express yourself in the same manner as your husband? As a wife who wants to meet her husband's needs, you need to understand the unspoken issues that are powerful symbols to your husband. As a wife, you are commanded to submit to your husband. Fulfill your roles as a wife and help him fulfill his roles as a husband. As you accept and fulfill your roles that God designed, you will function more effectively in those roles and better translate and interpret the actions and needs of your husband.